My Prayers

A Jewish child's book of prayers for every day

by Rabbi Barton G. Lee
and Rabbi Roy A. Walter

My Name

_____

My Prayers

A Jewish child's book of prayers for every day

by
Rabbi Barton G. Lee
and
Rabbi Roy A. Walter

illustrations by
Limb Design
based on drawings by Jose' Perez

published by
Congregation Emanu El
Houston, Texas
2011

ABOUT THE AUTHORS

Rabbi Barton G. Lee

Rabbi Barton G. Lee is the Rabbi/Executive Director of the Hillel Jewish Student Center at Arizona State University in Tempe, Arizona, and a Faculty Associate at ASU. He has served on the Liturgy Committee of the Central Conference of American Rabbis and has authored several liturgical publications. Rabbi Lee is married to Marcie Schoenberg Lee. They are the parents of Noam and Nira Lee.

Rabbi Roy A. Walter

Rabbi Roy A. Walter is Senior Rabbi of Congregation Emanu El, Houston, Texas, and a Faculty Associate at St. Thomas University, Houston, Texas. He has served on the Liturgy Committee of the Central Conference of American Rabbis and is author of the "For Younger Children" section of *Gates of Prayer for Young People*. Rabbi Walter is married to Linda Cohn Walter. They are the parents of Benjamin, Michel and Aaron Walter and grandparents of Ethan and Hannah Walter.

Dedication

Helen Pasternak touched the hearts and souls of all who knew her. She was kind, loving and generous with her time. Helen loved teaching Sunday School to the young first graders at Congregation Emanu El in Houston, Texas. When her twenty (20) years of teaching ended, her passion led her to reading stories to the children as they gathered around her rocking chair. She was everyone's *bubbie*.

"My Prayers" is a gift from Helen's family to children everywhere. It is our special way of honoring our mother and grandmother and continuing her tradition of love for children and for Judaism. Honoring her memory brings us peace that we have captured her spirit and shared her passions.

Mom, you remain forever in our hearts.

Cary, Matt and Jan

From the Authors to Adults

My Prayers is based on the authors' belief that God is near - that God cares about us, shares our joys and sorrows and is a source of strength in times of anxiety. We believe that prayer expresses deep personal feelings and is our way of sharing our joys, sorrows and anxieties with God.

Children are prayerful by nature, but they often need help giving expression to their spiritual feelings. *My Prayers* is designed for parents, grandparents, older siblings, caregivers, or baby-sitters to read with a child who doesn't yet read, and then, when the child learns how to read, to read for himself or herself.

We hope this book will become a regular and familiar part of a child's life. As children go to sleep and awaken, reading books is already part of their routine. We envision that reading *My Prayers* will become a daily occurrence in a child's life. When other books are chosen for reading, a prayer from *My Prayers* can serve as the last reading in the evening or the first in the morning, to create the habit of closing and opening each day with prayer.

The prayers in *My Prayers* give religious expression to experiences in a child's life. The Table of Contents enables the reader to choose the prayer or prayers that fit a mood or occasion the child is experiencing or reflects his or her interest.

You will note the *Sh'ma* is transliterated, but not translated. The usual translations are too abstract for young children. Jewish tradition teaches that these are the first Hebrew words we teach our children. So, when your child asks what the words of the *Sh'ma* mean, teach your child that these words are the Jewish way of saying, "We believe in One God."

These prayers may also be useful in stimulating conversation between adults and children. One might ask a child about his or her feelings before or after reading a prayer. Another idea would be to encourage a child to draw or dictate or write something expressing his or her own prayer.

We have alternated masculine and feminine pronouns, under the assumption that the reader will change genders as appropriate for each prayer.

We hope this book helps every child who experiences it to learn to pray, and enriches his or her conversations about God and religion.

Table of Contents

My prayer
about
going to sleep

When the sun sets,
the world looks different
and we do nighttime things.

People go home.

We clean up our toys.

And get ready for bed.

When I wake up tomorrow,
I will be ready to do daytime things again.
To run and jump and play.

But now it is time to go to sleep,
so my body can rest. And I can grow.

I know You are with me in the day
and in the night, God.

I pray that I will have a good night's sleep,
and be ready for a wonderful day tomorrow.

שְׁמַע יִשְׂרָאֵל יְיָ אֱלֹהֵינוּ יְיָ אֶחָד.
Sh'ma Yisrael Adonai Eloheinu Adonai Echad.

1

My prayer about home

There are lots of places I like to go.

To the park,
where I can run and swing and slide.
To the store,
where we buy food and clothes and toys.
To the restaurant,
where we eat pizza and apples and cookies.

But there is one place I love best of all,
my home.
Where I sleep and eat and play,
and I know where everything is.

My home is where I live with people I love.
They love me too.

At home I feel safe and warm,
and people take care of me.
Thank You, God, for wonderful places.
And for my home, the most special place of all.

שְׁמַע יִשְׂרָאֵל יְיָ אֱלֹהֵינוּ יְיָ אֶחָד.
Sh'ma Yisrael Adonai Eloheinu Adonai Echad.

I had a bad dream.
It scared me.
I'm glad
it wasn't real.

When I'm sleeping,
my body is resting.

But my mind is still at work.

Sometimes it imagines
happy thoughts
and pretty pictures.

Sometimes it imagines
frightening thoughts
and scary pictures.

I'm glad I woke up and
my bad dream is gone.

Help me to remember that
dreams are not real, God.
I'm glad that I am safe and
You are with me always.

שְׁמַע יִשְׂרָאֵל יְיָ אֱלֹהֵינוּ יְיָ אֶחָד.
Sh'ma Yisrael Adonai Eloheinu Adonai Echad.

3

My prayer about my birthday

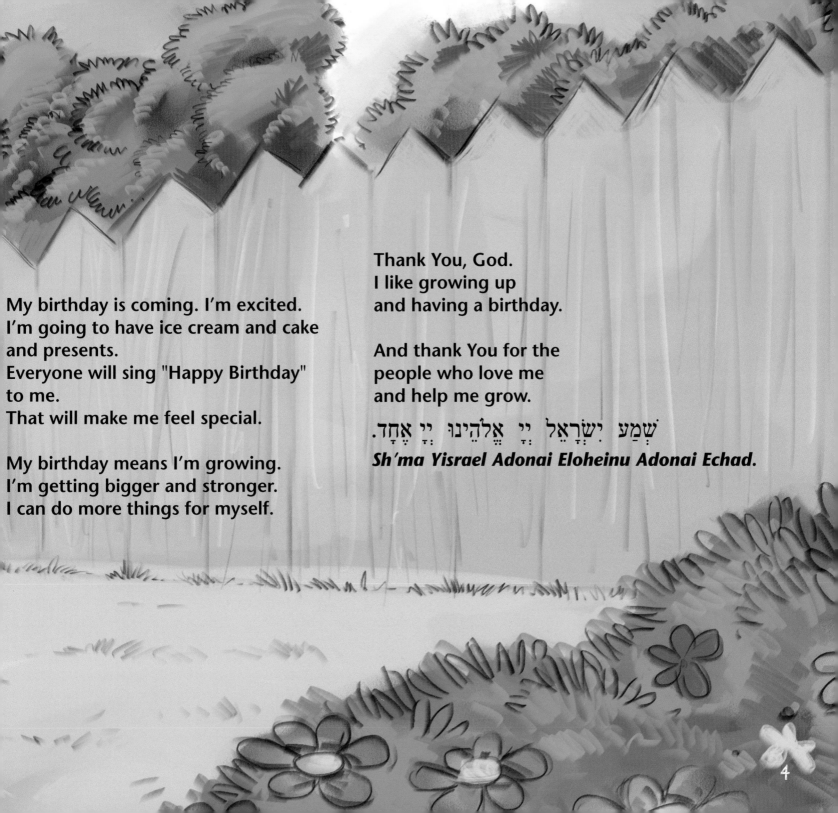

My birthday is coming. I'm excited.
I'm going to have ice cream and cake
and presents.
Everyone will sing "Happy Birthday"
to me.
That will make me feel special.

My birthday means I'm growing.
I'm getting bigger and stronger.
I can do more things for myself.

Thank You, God.
I like growing up
and having a birthday.

And thank You for the
people who love me
and help me grow.

שְׁמַע יִשְׂרָאֵל יְיָ אֱלֹהֵינוּ יְיָ אֶחָד.
Sh'ma Yisrael Adonai Eloheinu Adonai Echad.

4

My prayer about my pet

I love my pet _____.
I like to hold her and play with her.

I must be careful not to hurt her.
I can help take care of my pet.
She needs me to give her food and water
and love every day.

Thank You, God, for making a world
that has pets for us to love and care for.

שְׁמַע יִשְׂרָאֵל יְיָ אֱלֹהֵינוּ יְיָ אֶחָד.
Sh'ma Yisrael Adonai Eloheinu Adonai Echad.

5

My prayer about **not feeling well**

I don't feel very well tonight.
I didn't feel good all day.

It's not fun to be sick.
Sometimes I get a tummy ache.
Sometimes I have to blow my nose a lot.
Sometimes my ear hurts.

I want to feel better so I can
go to school,
play outside,
and be with my friends.

Sleep will help me feel better.
The people who love me
help me feel better too.

I know You love me, God,
and will help me feel better soon.

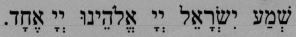

שְׁמַע יִשְׂרָאֵל יְיָ אֱלֹהֵינוּ יְיָ אֶחָד.
Sh'ma Yisrael Adonai Eloheinu Adonai Echad.

6

My prayer

about

my new home

I am excited to be in my new home
and sleep in my new room.
We brought lots of things with
us from our old house.
I am glad they are here with me.

I will miss my old house and my old neighborhood.
I will remember my friends, and
I hope I see them again soon.

In my new house it will
be fun to find new
games to play.

New places to hide.
And new things to do.

I will make new
friends, and
we can share our
books and toys.

Thank You, God, for
old places and for new places.

Thank You, especially for the people I love
who make my home so special.

שְׁמַע יִשְׂרָאֵל יְיָ אֱלֹהֵינוּ יְיָ אֶחָד.
Sh'ma Yisrael Adonai Eloheinu Adonai Echad.

7

My prayer
about

a rainbow

The sky was beautiful after the rain today.
The dark clouds went away, the sun came out,
and I saw a rainbow.
Its bright colors made me happy.

Rainbows are a gift from You, God.

They are a sign that You care about us
        and will always be with us.

Thank You, God, for the rain
that waters the earth,
and for the beautiful rainbow
that follows.

שְׁמַע יִשְׂרָאֵל יְיָ אֱלֹהֵינוּ יְיָ אֶחָד.
Sh'ma Yisrael Adonai Eloheinu Adonai Echad.

8

My prayer

about

my dog that died

I loved my dog _____.

He was my friend.
We did lots of things together.
We played and ran and chased each other.
He would lick my nose,
and we would roll in the grass.

I am sad my dog died.

I will remember him
for a long time.

I miss him very much.

Thank You, God,
for animals
that can be pets.

I like living in a
world where
pets can be loved
by people.

שְׁמַע יִשְׂרָאֵל יְיָ אֱלֹהֵינוּ יְיָ אֶחָד.
Sh'ma Yisrael Adonai Eloheinu
Adonai Echad.

My prayer
about
going to a new school

Soon I will be going to a new school.
I am excited and scared at the same time.

There are so many things to learn:
    Where my classroom is.
    Who my teacher will be.
    Who the other kids are.
I hope I will like it there.

Starting a new school
is part of growing up.
I know about so many things now,
and I want to learn even more.

I can't wait to read new books.
Work on the computer.
And make new things with
paint and glue and clay.

Thank You, God, for questions
and answers that help me learn
more about the world.

שְׁמַע יִשְׂרָאֵל יְיָ אֱלֹהֵינוּ יְיָ אֶחָד.
Sh'ma Yisrael Adonai Eloheinu
Adonai Echad.

10

My prayer about a bad day

At times I wasn't very happy today.
Some things didn't go right.

I didn't do some of the things
I was supposed to.

And some people weren't
very nice to me.

I tried to be good, but it didn't work.
I tried to be helpful, but no one paid
attention to me.

This kind of day happens sometimes.
I hope tomorrow is a better day.

Are there days when the world makes
You unhappy, God, and people don't pay
attention to You?

I'm saying this prayer to tell You
I care about You.
And I know You care about me too.

שְׁמַע יִשְׂרָאֵל יְיָ אֱלֹהֵינוּ יְיָ אֶחָד.
Sh'ma Yisrael Adonai Eloheinu Adonai Echad.

11

Thank You, God, for a wonderful day.
For the pretty sounds I heard.
The bright colors I saw.

And the good
foods I ate.

For the happy things I did.
The fun games I played.
And the new things I learned.

For friends I like.
And family I love.

Thank You, God, for surprises.
The ones I find in the world.
And the ones I discover in my head.

You are wonderful, God, for making a world
with so many things to make us happy.

שְׁמַע יִשְׂרָאֵל יְיָ אֱלֹהֵינוּ יְיָ אֶחָד.
Sh'ma Yisrael Adonai Eloheinu Adonai Echad.

12

My prayer

about

doing something bad

I did something today
I shouldn't have done.

Everyone does bad things sometimes
which make other people unhappy.

Then we should say, "I'm sorry,"
and try not to do it again.

When I say, "I'm sorry," and mean it,
and try not to do it again,
people will forgive me.
And You will forgive me too, God.

Thank You, for making a world where
we can be forgiven when we do
something bad.

שְׁמַע יִשְׂרָאֵל יְיָ אֱלֹהֵינוּ יְיָ אֶחָד.
Sh'ma Yisrael Adonai Eloheinu
Adonai Echad.

13

My prayer
about
my new baby

Finally my new baby is here.

Everybody is excited.

I am happy, too.
(I felt her move inside Mommy's tummy,
and now I am able to see her.)

She is very small and cries a lot.

She can't do anything for herself, so all of us have to
take care of her.

I have to be careful not to hurt her,
but I can kiss and hug her gently.
I can't wait until she is big like I am.
Then we can run and laugh and play together.

I love my new
baby, God.
And I know You love
her, too.

Help us both to grow and
be healthy and happy.

שְׁמַע יִשְׂרָאֵל יְיָ אֱלֹהֵינוּ יְיָ אֶחָד.
*Sh'ma Yisrael Adonai
Eloheinu Adonai Echad.*

14

My prayer

about

a new day

The sun is up, and I am awake.

My eyes are open.

I am ready to read my books.

Play computer games.

Watch TV.

And be with my family and friends.

There are so many wonderful things I can do today, God.

I'm glad I am awake and ready to do them.

Thank You for this new day. And for lots of things to see and hear and do.

שְׁמַע יִשְׂרָאֵל יְיָ אֱלֹהֵינוּ יְיָ אֶחָד.
Sh'ma Yisrael Adonai Eloheinu Adonai Echad.

My prayer
about
going on a trip

I'm so excited!
We're going on a trip.

I don't know which books and
toys to take with me,
but I know I can't
take everything.

When we get there,
I will have lots of fun.

I can play new games.

See new things.

And meet new people.

When I come back, I will be happy
to see my home and my friends
again.

You are everywhere, God.

I know You will be with me while
I am on my trip
and when I come home.

שְׁמַע יִשְׂרָאֵל יְיָ אֱלֹהֵינוּ יְיָ אֶחָד.
*Sh'ma Yisrael Adonai Eloheinu
Adonai Echad.*

I can hardly wait to get started.
The trip will take a long time.
I will have to work at being good.

My prayer about being afraid of a storm

The thunder is so loud the house shakes.

The rain is beating on the roof.
And the lightning jumps out of the dark.

I am afraid,
but I don't have to be.

I am safe in my home with
someone I love near me.
I'm glad she is here.
Even when she leaves,
I can still feel safe.

I am never alone.
You are always with me, God;
I don't need to be afraid.

שְׁמַע יִשְׂרָאֵל יְיָ אֱלֹהֵינוּ יְיָ אֶחָד.
Sh'ma Yisrael Adonai Eloheinu Adonai Echad.

My prayer about being sick in the hospital

When I go to the hospital, the doctors and nurses will be there to help me.

They want me to be healthy.

And they want to help me feel better.

I must be brave, since I will be in a strange place.
Being brave is part of growing up.
It's hard, but I'm going to do it.

People I love will be with me and help me be brave.

I know You will be with me too, God.
Please, help me be brave and get well.

שְׁמַע יִשְׂרָאֵל יְיָ אֱלֹהֵינוּ יְיָ אֶחָד.
Sh'ma Yisrael Adonai Eloheinu Adonai Echad.

My prayer

about

the death of someone I love

_____ died and I am very sad.

Other people are very sad, too.

Some of us have been crying.

We loved him.

I wish I could see him again.
But I can always remember
all the wonderful things about him.
And how much we loved each other.

I will miss him.

In a little while I will be able to think
about him without being so sad.

Thank You, God, for _____.
I will remember him.

And I know that You will, too.

שְׁמַע יִשְׂרָאֵל יְיָ אֱלֹהֵינוּ יְיָ אֶחָד.
Sh'ma Yisrael Adonai Eloheinu Adonai Echad.

19

My prayer
about
someone I love
being sick

_____ is sick, and I want her to get well.

I know that everyone gets sick sometimes.

But I don't like it when someone I love gets sick.

I'm glad there are doctors

and nurses

and medicines

to help people get better.

I want my visit to help make

_____ get better.

She needs Your help too, God.

Please help her get well.

שְׁמַע יִשְׂרָאֵל יְיָ אֱלֹהֵינוּ יְיָ אֶחָד.
Sh'ma Yisrael Adonai Eloheinu Adonai Echad.

My prayer

about

learning

I like to learn, God,

where clouds come from,
why it rains sometimes,
how to read and count and draw.

Who invented writing?
What makes flowers grow?
When will I be big?

I have lots of questions.

They begin with

who and what,
when and where,
why and how.

Some things I can understand now.
Others I will understand as I grow up.

Some questions have easy answers.

Other questions I'll have to think about.

I like to learn, God.

Thank You for giving me a mind to think up lots of questions and to try to find answers.

שְׁמַע יִשְׂרָאֵל יְיָ אֱלֹהֵינוּ יְיָ אֶחָד.
Sh'ma Yisrael Adonai Eloheinu Adonai Echad.

My prayer
about
someone I love
going on a trip

_____ has gone on a trip,
and I wish he didn't have to go.

I will miss him when he is gone.

I hope the time passes quickly until
he comes back.

During the day, I don't miss him so much.

I am busy. I go to school. Watch TV.
And play with my friends.

But at bedtime, I miss him most.

I like when we talk
and hug and kiss good night.

I am thinking of him now,
and know he misses me too.

Thank You, God, for
_____'s love,

which I feel when he is here
and when he is away.

שְׁמַע יִשְׂרָאֵל יְיָ אֱלֹהֵינוּ יְיָ אֶחָד.
Sh'ma Yisrael Adonai Eloheinu
Adonai Echad.

My prayer

about

friends

I like my friends.

We have fun together.

We go outdoors.
Share our toys.
Play computer
games together.

We can call each other on the phone
and talk about lots of things.

I like to have good friends.
I like to be a good friend too.

Friends are very
special people.

Thank You, God, for making a world
where people can be friends
and share things together.

שְׁמַע יִשְׂרָאֵל יְיָ אֱלֹהֵינוּ יְיָ אֶחָד.

Sh'ma Yisrael Adonai Eloheinu Adonai Echad.

My prayer

about

how wonderful the world is

I keep thinking how wonderful the world is.

There's the sun that shines during the day.
And the moon and stars at night.

I love summer when I can swim.
And fall when the leaves change color.

I love winter when the trees are bare.
And spring when the flowers bloom.

I love holidays with special foods to eat.
And songs to sing.
And stories to tell.

New things are always happening.

I see and hear and touch and feel them every day.

Thank You, God, for making such a wonderful world.

שְׁמַע יִשְׂרָאֵל יְיָ אֱלֹהֵינוּ יְיָ אֶחָד.
Sh'ma Yisrael Adonai Eloheinu Adonai Echad.

24

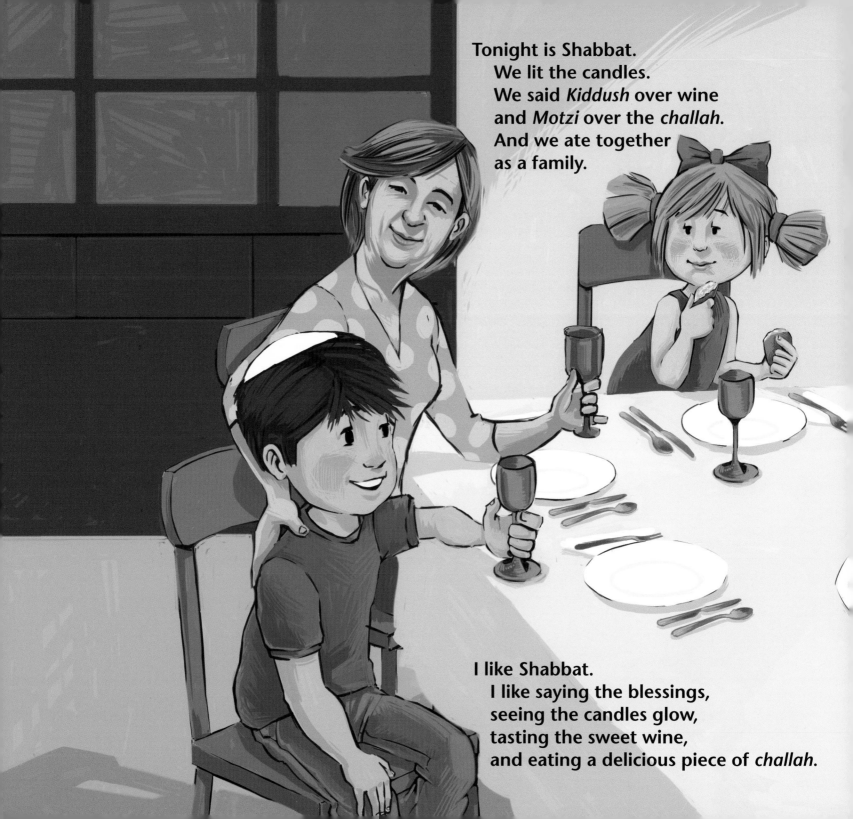

Tonight is Shabbat.
We lit the candles.
We said *Kiddush* over wine
and *Motzi* over the *challah*.
And we ate together
as a family.

I like Shabbat.
I like saying the blessings,
seeing the candles glow,
tasting the sweet wine,
and eating a delicious piece of *challah*.

I especially like being with my family on Shabbat.

I like the warm feeling I get when we are together.

Thank You, God, for giving us this very special day.

שְׁמַע יִשְׂרָאֵל יְיָ אֱלֹהֵינוּ יְיָ אֶחָד.
Sh'ma Yisrael Adonai Eloheinu Adonai Echad.

25

Acknowledgements

We would like to express our deep gratitude to:

Jan Pasternak, first and foremost, a member of Congregation Emanu El, Houston, TX and graduate of ASU, without whose patience, dedication, and perseverance this book would not have come to fruition. Her humor and gracious spirit are very much a part of this book. It has been a joy to work with her over the years.

José Perez, whose original drawings form the basis for the artwork in this book.

Linda Limb of Limb Design and her staff, for their creativity in bringing the artwork and layout to final form. Linda's many helpful suggestions have enhanced the book from cover to cover.

Brenda Nasser, for faithfully keeping up with the text over many years as it has gone through countless revisions.

Myra Lipper, who first brought to Jan Pasternak the idea of publishing this book in Jan's mother's memory.

Adie Marks, for his enthusiasm for this book and for leading us to José Perez.

Dr. Jacob Petuchowski, may his memory be for a blessing, who taught us the art of liturgy and inspired us to offer children the experience of personal prayer.

Our wives Marcie and Linda, for their patience, encouragement and insistence that we finish this project.

Our children Noam and Nira Lee and Benjamin, Michel and Aaron Walter whose existence inspired us to begin this project and who grew up faster than we created. Hopefully, it will be used by their children.